D0100440

MY BEAR
I WISH . . . DO YOU?

My Bear is an irresistible teddy bear
sure to capture the hearts of young readers
and listeners. Each page shows him engaged
in a familiar activity and is accompanied
by a rhyme that is simple, memorable, and
filled with fun. And because every rhyme
ends with a question that cries out for
an answer, here is the perfect book for
parents to read with their eager children!

MY BEAR
I WISH . . . DO YOU?

Written by Ruth Thomson
Illustrated by Ian Beck

TREASURE PRESS

I wish I were bold
like those brave knights of old
who had banners of gold.
Do you?

I wish I could be
a fine sailor at sea
and catch lobster for tea.
Do you?

I wish I could camp
with a tent and a lamp
and feel snug in the damp.
Do you?

I wish I could fly
through the clouds in the sky
and watch birds flying by.
Do you?

I wish I could glue
some bark and bamboo
to make a canoe.
Do you?

I wish I could go
for a sledge in the snow
with a heigh and a ho.
Do you?

I wish I could track
with my clothes in a pack
and bring fierce tigers back.

Do you?

I wish, for a dare,
I could stand on a chair
with my legs in the air.
Do you?

I wish, very soon,
I could fly to the moon
and dig holes with a spoon.

Do you?

I wish I were quick
at doing a trick
with three cups and a chick.

Do you?

I wish I were king
with a robe and a ring
and a dog that could sing.
Do you?

I wish I could make
an extraordinary cake
which took no time to bake.
Do you?

First published in Great Britain in 1986 by
Conran Octopus Limited

This edition first published in Great Britain in 1990 by
Treasure Press
Michelin House
81 Fulham Road
London SW3 6RB

Copyright © Conran Octopus Limited 1986

All rights reserved

Designed by Heather Garioch

ISBN 1 85051 309 0

Printed in the UK